SCIENCE PROJECTS

ROCKS AND SOILS

Robert Snedden

Photography by
Chris Fairclough

WAYLAND

Produced for Wayland Publishers Ltd by
Discovery Books Ltd
Unit 3, 37 Watling Street, Leintwardine
Shropshire SY7 0LW, England

First published in 1998 by
Wayland Publishers Ltd
61 Western Road, Hove
East Sussex BN3 1JD, England

British Library Cataloguing in Publication Data
Snedden, Robert. -
    Rocks and soils (Science projects)
    1. Rocks - Juvenile literature
    2. Soils - Juvenile literature
    I. Title
    552
ISBN 0 7502 2152 6

Printed and bound in Italy by
G. Canale & C.S.p.A., Turin

Designer: Ian Winton
Editor: Sabrina Crewe
Consultant: Jeremy Bloomfield
Illustrations: Julian Baker: front cover;
Stefan Chabluk: pages 8, 10, 17, 22, 38, 40;
Jeremy Gower: pages 6, 15.

Picture acknowledgements:
The publishers would like to thank the following
for permission to reproduce their pictures:
Bruce Coleman: pages 4, 26, 30, 31, 36, 42;
Ecoscene: page 44; **Getty Images**: front cover,
pages 5, 12, 18, 35, 39; **Robert Harding**: page 28;
NASA: page 7; **Oxford Scientific Films**: page 32;
Science Photo Library: pages 11, 13, 14, 24, 29.

The publishers would like to thank the staff and
pupils of **Harborne Junior School, Birmingham,**
for their help in the preparation of this book.

Find Wayland on the internet at
http://www.wayland.co.uk

NATIONAL CURRICULUM NOTES

The investigations in this book are cross-referenced to Programmes of Study for Science and
Geography at Key Stages (KS) 2 and 3.

A ROCKY WORLD Materials and their properties; grouping
and classifying materials; describing and grouping rocks and
soils. Science KS2 Sc3 1a
INSIDE THE EARTH, THE CRUST, THE ACTIVE EARTH,
MOUNTAIN BUILDING and **VOLCANOES** Global distribution
of earthquakes and volcanoes; relationship with crustal
plate boundaries; nature, cause and effect of earthquakes.
Geography KS3 Thematic Studies 7
MINERALS Elements and compounds, Science KS3 Sc3 1
IGNEOUS ROCK The rock cycle; igneous processes;
classification of igneous rocks. Science KS3 Sc3 2g & 2h
METAMORPHIC ROCK The rock cycle; metamorphic
processes; classification of metamorphic rocks. Science KS3
Sc3 2g & 2h
SEDIMENTARY ROCK The rock cycle; sedimentary
processes; classification of sedimentary rocks. Science KS3
Sc3 2g & 2h
FOSSILS The formation of fossils in sedimentary rock.
ROCK RESOURCES Relating properties of materials to their
everyday uses. Science KS2 Sc3 1a

METEORITES Introduction to extraterrestial rocks
WEATHERING and **EROSION** How rocks are weathered by
expansion and contraction and by freezing; how acids in the
atmosphere lead to chemical weathering of rock. Geography
KS3 Thematic Studies 8; Science KS3 Sc3 2f and 3i
FROM ROCK TO SOIL Separating soil particles by sieving.
Science KS2 Sc3 3a
THE LIVING EARTH Identifying plants and animals.
Science KS3 Sc2 4c
SOIL PROFILES Describing the characteristics of soils.
Science KS2 Sc3 1d
SOIL GROUPS How vegetation is related to soil; describing
the characteristics of soils. Geography KS3 Thematic Studies
10; Science KS2 Sc3 1d
NATURAL GARDENERS How plants and animals are suited
to their environment. Science KS2 Sc2 5b
THE HUMAN FACTOR The effect of human activity on
soils and ecosystems. Geography KS3 Thematic Studies 10

CONTENTS

A ROCKY WORLD

Over four billion years ago the Solar System, consisting of the Sun and its family of planets, took shape from a cloud of interstellar dust. Giant gas planets – Jupiter, Saturn, Uranus and Neptune – formed in its outer reaches. Closer to the infant Sun, the rocky planets – Mercury, Venus, Mars and our own Earth – formed.

The young Earth was an inhospitable place of bubbling molten lava. It was heated by radiation from within and bombarded by meteorites night and day. Over millions of years, the interior of the planet separated into layers. A rocky crust formed on the surface, like the skin that forms on the top of warmed milk.

The Earth's rocky crust, on which we live, can be covered by fields, woodland and houses. It can rise up in the form of bare mountain peaks, or plunge deep into canyons, such as this one in Colorado in the United States of America. Much of the Earth's rock surface remains unseen beneath oceans.

Those first ancient rocks are long vanished, transformed into other forms by erosion, heat and pressure. Rocks that dinosaurs passed by have been broken down by wind and water. They have become part of the Earth's soil cover, supporting life on the land. This book tells the story of the Earth's rocks and soils. It is a story that continues today and will never end, so long as the Earth exists.

TAKE A ROCK WALK

MATERIALS
● a notepad and pencil

Wherever you are, in the city or in the country, you will find rocks all around. The kerbstones that line your streets may very well be made of granite, originally a molten rock that cooled deep beneath the ground. The walls of some buildings might be made of sandstone, a rock that formed gradually over millions of years from the compacting together of many tiny fragments. Look inside the bank and you might find marble used for counters and floors.

Take a walk through your town and try to spot different types of rock that have been used in the buildings. Your library will have books for identifying rocks.

INSIDE THE EARTH

At the centre of the Earth is a hot, dense inner core of solid iron and nickel. Around this is the outer core, which consists of molten iron and nickel. The core is surrounded by the mantle, a layer of thick rock that is partly molten and partly solid. Finally, over the mantle, is the part we know best – the Earth's crust, upon which we live. Nobody has ever seen below the Earth's crust, but a picture of the inside of the Earth has been built up by careful scientific study.

A big earthquake sends vibrations, or waves, racing through the Earth. These shock waves are known as seismic waves. As the waves encounter different materials they change direction, change

speed, or are stopped altogether. Some seismic waves travel through both solids and liquids, and some only through solids. By observing the speed and direction of seismic waves, scientists have been able to construct a model of the Earth's interior.

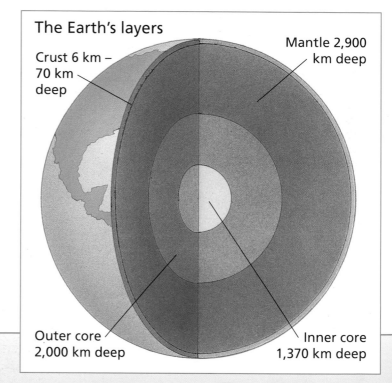

The Earth's layers

Crust 6 km – 70 km deep

Mantle 2,900 km deep

Outer core 2,000 km deep

Inner core 1,370 km deep

EARTH MODEL

1. Ask an adult carefully to cut out a segment from the rubber ball so that it looks like the picture of the inside of the Earth shown in the diagram.

2. Using the diagram above as a guide, cut out coloured circles for the mantle, the inner core and the outer core, and stick them together to form one circle with three rings.

3. Cut the circle in half, and glue the halves into place on the ball.

MATERIALS
- a green or blue foam ball
- a modelling knife
- string
- coloured card
- coloured pens
- glue

Photographs taken from space, such as this one, show us the surface of the Earth. But this is only a thin skin over what lies below. The seething layers of the mantle and core cannot be seen.

4. Draw blue oceans or green continents on the outside of the model Earth, depending on the colour of your ball.

5. Glue one end of the string to your model and hang it from the ceiling.

Did you know?

At the foot of the world's deepest mineshaft, in South Africa, temperatures can reach 50°C. The temperature at the centre of the Earth is probably about 3-4,000°C.

THE CRUST

Although it is by far the thinnest of the layers that make up the Earth, the crust is the most important to us. This is where we live. The crust can be divided into two types.

The continental crust is composed largely of granite and is between 30 and 70 km deep. It is at its deepest under mountain ranges. The oldest rocks of the continental crust are over 3,000 million years old.

The oceanic crust is made of relatively young rocks, a mere 200 million years old on average. It is largely composed of basalt, one of the commonest

volcanic rocks. Basalt is usually dark grey in colour, but may also be green and brown. The oceanic crust is on average 10 km thick.

The distribution of material on the surface of the Earth is always changing. Over millions of years, mountains are very gradually worn down. The weight of the crust at that point is lessened and the crust rises up. The material worn from the mountains gathers somewhere else (at the bottom of the sea, perhaps), causing the crust there to sink because it is heavier. These balancing rises and falls in the crust are called isostasy.

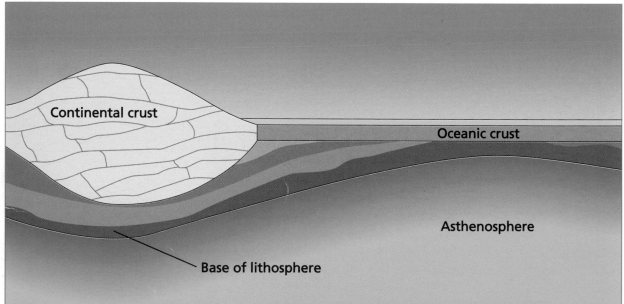

Continental crust

Oceanic crust

Asthenosphere

Base of lithosphere

The crust, together with the upper layer of the mantle, forms the rigid lithosphere. Between 80 and 160 km beneath the crust there is a zone of molten rock, the lower part of the mantle, called the asthenosphere. The lithosphere is constantly moving as it floats on top of the liquid asthenosphere, rising and falling slowly as the weight of the crust changes at different points on the surface.

AN ISOSTATIC MODEL

The massive sheets of ice that form during an Ice age place a great deal of extra weight on the crust beneath them. After an ice age, the part of the crust that was under the ice slowly rises up again. Parts of Scandinavia are still rising at the rate of one centimetre a year, ten thousand years after the last ice age ended!

1. Fill the container with enough water in which to float the wooden block, and put the block into the water. The wood represents a section of the crust and the water is the asthenosphere.

2. Carefully note how far up the block the water comes. The block doesn't rise and fall in the water. It is balanced. A mountain is balanced in the same way, with a rock 'root' extending down into the asthenosphere.

3. Now it is time for an ice age! Carefully put some ice cubes on top of the block. The extra weight on the crust makes it sink lower into the asthenosphere.

4. Let the ice melt. What happens to the level of the wood?

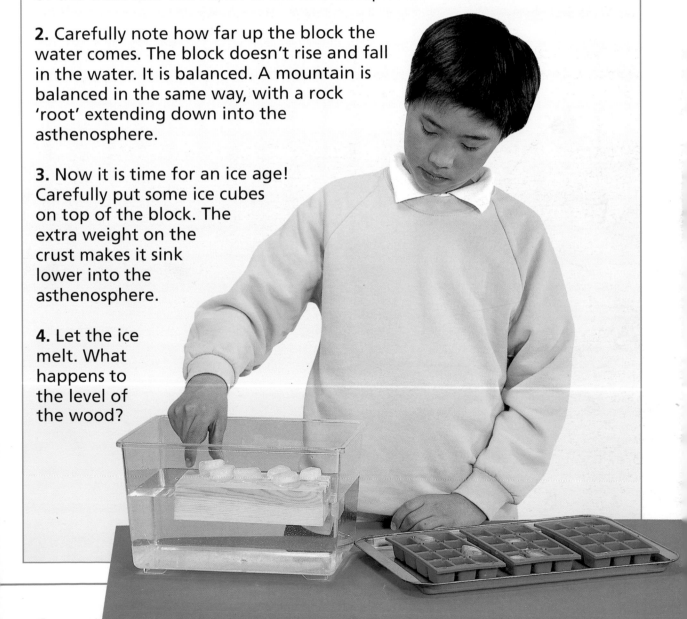

THE ACTIVE EARTH

The Earth's crust is not a single solid sheet. It is made up of a number of continually moving slabs, or plates, that float on the molten mantle. Liquid rock from below, heated by the core, rises up through the mantle. At the same time cooler, denser rock sinks down. The result is a very slow, circular current travelling through the mantle. This current carries the floating plates along on the surface, like suitcases on an airport conveyor belt.

When plates collide, one plate can sometimes be forced underneath the other. The crust of the sinking plate melts into the Earth's mantle. Molten rock rises and melts through the crust above it, causing volcanoes. When plates crack and move apart, they allow molten rock to rise up between them. This is happening in the middle of the Atlantic Ocean.

Sometimes, as the plates slide past each other, they can become stuck for a while. Then something gives way and they get moving again suddenly. The result can be a massive earthquake, which sends huge vibrations through the crust. Large-scale movements of the crust, particularly along the boundaries

A PANGAEAN PUZZLE

Take a look in an atlas. Can you see how neatly the west coast of Africa would fit around the east coast of South America? Scientists believe that 300 million years ago the Earth's landmasses gathered together in one supercontinent, called Pangaea. (The pale green areas show the land that joined the continents together.) It is thought that Pangaea began to split apart again about 200 million years ago.

MATERIALS
- an atlas or world map
- tracing paper
- a pencil
- a pair of scissors
- coloured card or paper in various colours

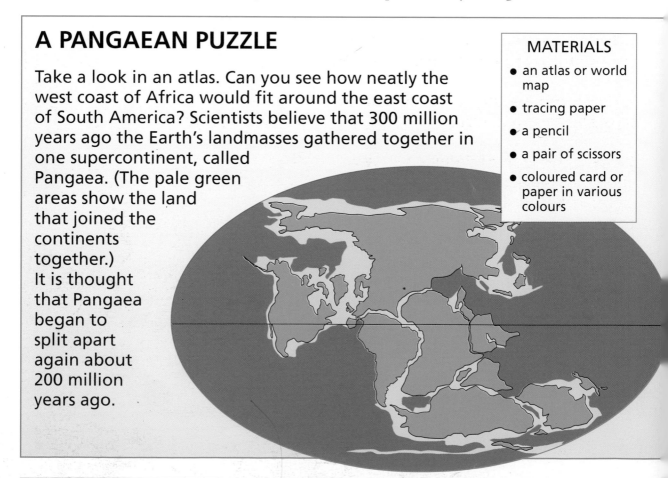

of plates, puts a huge amount of strain on the rocks. Eventually, if enough pressure builds up, the rocks pass their breaking point, and a crack, or fault, opens up.

The results of the 1989 earthquake in San Francisco, USA. Thousands of earthquakes take place every day, but only the biggest few are felt. A major earthquake can cause landslides and avalanches, and open up cracks in the ground. The ground can be lifted by several metres, causing severe damage to buildings and other constructions.

1. Trace around all the continents and Greenland on a large map of the world.

2. Copy your tracings on to coloured card and cut them out.

3. Using the map of Pangaea shown opposite, see if you can fit your pieces together to form the ancient supercontinent. You will need to cut India and the Arabian Peninsula from the bottom of Asia to make your puzzle work.

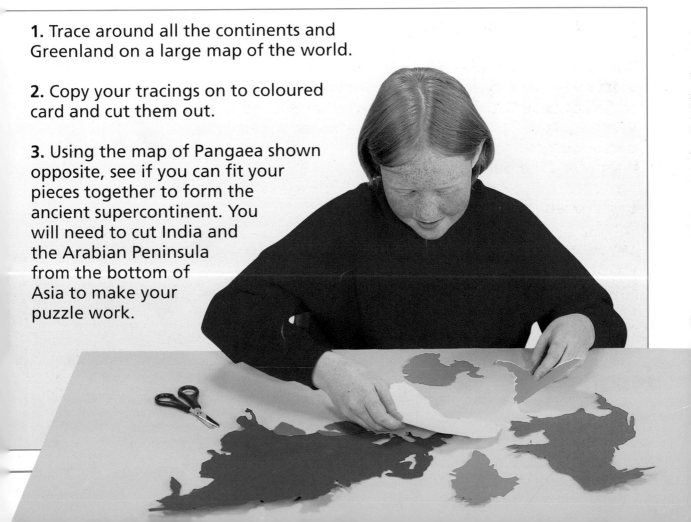

MOUNTAIN BUILDING

When two plates carrying continental crust collide, the rocks are squeezed and buckled to form mountains. These are called fold mountains, because of the folding of the crust that takes place.

Block mountains are formed by the movement of huge masses of rock up or down along cracks, or faults, in the Earth's surface. Block mountains usually have steep cliffs. The shifts in the crust that form block mountains can also give rise to earthquakes.

Volcanic mountains form when plates collide at the edge of continents. Dome mountains are also made by volcanic activity. Molten rock pushes up the crust from below, producing rounded shapes like blisters on the Earth's surface. The domes are full of hot liquid rock when they are first formed. Ancient dome mountains can be seen in the Auvergne region of France.

The greatest of the Earth's mountain ranges are the undersea ranges that reach up from the floors of the oceans. The longest mountain range in the world is the mid-Atlantic Ridge, beneath the Atlantic Ocean.

The highest mountains in the world, the Himalayas, were once at the bottom of an ocean. They were folded upwards over millions of years as the plate carrying India collided with the Asian plate.

MAKE A MOUNTAIN RANGE

MATERIALS
● Modelling clay in four or five different colours

1. Make several long strips of the same size with the modelling clay, one of each colour. Make the strips as long as possible to get the most complex mountain range.

2. Place the layers on top of each other to represent layers of rock.

3. Slowly slide the layers together so that the middle begins to buckle. You may need a friend to push one end while you push the other.

See how the layers of your 'crust' fold up. This is what happens when plates collide and the land is forced upwards. Some layers may even fold right over so that they get jumbled. Layers that were underneath may end up on top. This is often found in real mountains.

The pattern in these layers of rock has clearly been made by the effects of folding. The rock was put under intense pressure as plates collided.

VOLCANOES

Most of the Earth's volcanoes are found in regions called volcanic belts. These belts mark the edges of the tectonic plates that make up the Earth's crust. The biggest belt of active volcanoes is the 'Ring of Fire' around the Pacific Ocean. Volcanoes are also found along the underwater mountain ranges such as the Mid-Atlantic Ridge where magma (molten rock) oozes out in regions where plates are moving apart.

A volcano occurs where there is an opening in the Earth's crust through which magma from below can pour out on to the surface as lava. Large amounts of gas are trapped in the magma. When it comes close to the surface, the pressure of the gases can blow a hole through any weakness in the crust. Vast quantities of dust and ashes may be blasted into the air by the force of the escaping gas. Not all volcanoes produce gas and ash, however: some just pour out lava.

The largest volcano on Earth is Mauna Loa in the Hawaiian Islands. The mountain measures 119 km across its base and is 4,170 m high. The lava from its frequent eruptions can flow to as far as 80 km away.

The heat inside the magma chamber below the Earth's crust pushes magma up the main vent of a volcano. It shoots out of the top of the volcano in the form of lava.

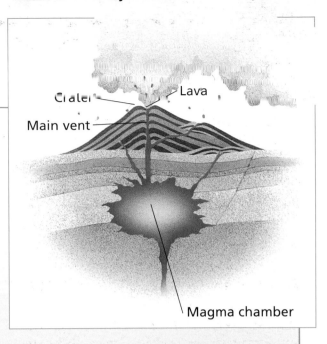

Crater

Lava

Main vent

Magma chamber

A BAKING SODA ERUPTION

1. Pour the washing up liquid, bicarbonate of soda, water and food colouring into the bottle, using the funnel if necesssary. Put the lid on the bottle.

2. Put the bottle on the tray or in the bowl.

3. Pile the sand around the bottle to make the sides of your volcano. Keep the top of the jar free.

4. Take the lid off carefully and put it to one side.

5. Pour the vinegar into the bottle and watch the eruption! See how your red "magma" flows down the "volcano".

MATERIALS

- sand
- 50 ml water
- 50 ml vinegar
- 50 ml bicarbonate of soda
- two tablespoons of washing up liquid
- red food colouring
- a tray or large bowl
- a glass or plastic bottle with a lid
- a funnel
- a measuring jug
- a tablespoon

MINERALS

Rocks are combinations of various minerals that have been formed by heat or pressure in the Earth. A mineral is a chemical element or compound found in or on the Earth. Salt, quartz, metals and even ice are all examples of minerals.

Every mineral is made by combining some of the 92 chemical elements that occur in nature. A mineral is always made up of the same chemical elements, combined in the same way. Quartz, for example, is always made up only of the elements silicon and oxygen. Gold, being an element itself, consists of nothing but atoms of gold. Some rocks are made up of only one mineral: marble, for instance, is made of calcite. Others may contain many minerals: granite is made up of quartz, mica and feldspar.

Minerals have a large variety of characteristics. The lustre of a mineral describes the way it shines in the light. A metallic lustre is shiny like the surface of a metal. A nonmetallic lustre can look, for example, like glass, like silk or like a pearl. Some minerals have no shine at all and are described as dull.

GROWING CRYSTALS

Minerals almost always form crystals. A crystal is a combination of atoms that join together to form a definite, orderly shape. Crystals form when minerals that have been melted or dissolved become solid again. It is easy and fun to grow your own crystals.

MATERIALS
- powdered alum
- food colouring
- hot water
- a saucer
- a glass jar
- some thread
- a pencil or small stick

1. Put one heaped teaspoon of alum in the jar. Add 2-3 tablespoons of hot water, and stir until the powder has dissolved.

2. Pour the dissolved alum into the saucer and leave it for about twelve hours. Keep it uncovered so that the water can evaporate.

Mohs' Scale of Hardness

In 1812, Friedrich Mohs, a German scientist, devised a hardness scale in which he listed ten minerals from the softest (talc) to the hardest (diamond). Each mineral in the scale can scratch those with a lower number, or be scratched by something higher up the scale.

Talc (1) and gypsum (2) can be scratched by a fingernail, which has a hardness of 2.5.

Calcite (3) can be scratched by a copper coin, which has a hardness of 3.5.

Fluorite (4) and apatite (5) can be scratched by a steel blade, which has a hardness of 5.5.

Orthoclase (6), topaz (7), quartz (8) and corundum (9) can scratch a steel blade.

Diamond (10) is about 40 times harder than talc, and can scratch all common materials.

3. When the water has evaporated, you will see crystals of alum left behind on the saucer. Select one of the largest crystals and carefully tie the thread around it. Tie the other end of the thread to a pencil or small stick.

4. Make up some more alum solution in the jar, using about four heaped teaspoons of alum, and filling the jar about two thirds full of hot water. Add a few drops of food colouring.

5. Hang the thread with the crystal inside the jar. Rest the pencil across the top of the jar to keep the crystal in position, submerged in the alum solution.

6. Leave the crystal for a few days and watch it grow!

IGNEOUS ROCK

Igneous means relating to fire. Igneous rocks are formed when the molten magma that lies under the Earth's crust rises to cooler regions either on or just beneath the surface, where it solidifies. Igneous rocks were the first to be formed when the young Earth began to cool, about 4 to 4.5 billion years ago.

When the magma becomes solid before reaching the surface, it forms what are known as intrusive igneous rocks. Intrusive rocks often cool slowly, tending to have large crystals. A mass of igneous rock formed inside the Earth is called a pluton. Millions of years may pass before the crust above the cooled magma has been worn away sufficiently to expose the pluton to view.

Basalt is a typical extrusive igneous rock. It forms much of the land surface of Iceland and the Deccan plateau in central India. The Giant's Causeway in Northern Ireland, seen here, is a remarkable example of basalt, where the lava cooled to form hexagonal columns.

VOLCANIC ROCK IN THE BATHROOM

There might be a piece of volcanic rock in your home, in the form of a pumice stone. Pumice is often ejected from a volcano during an eruption. It forms from the frothy scum on a lava flow that has gas bubbles trapped in it, and is a very light rock. People use pumice stones to scrub stains on their skin that won't come off with soap and water.

When lava solidifies on the Earth's surface after a volcanic eruption, it forms a type of igneous rock called extrusive igneous rock. Igneous rocks that form on the Earth's surface tend to cool very quickly, forming crystals that are often microscopically small. Obsidian, a dark glass-like rock, is formed from rapidly cooling lava.

Granite

LOOKING AT GRANITE

Granite is a good example of an intrusive igneous rock, and is found in many parts of the world. Because it has cooled slowly in the crust, it has very coarse grains. Pumice is an extrusive igneous rock with fine grains.

MATERIALS
- a granite sample
- a pumice stone
- a magnifying glass

1. Compare the granite sample to the pumice stone. What are the obvious differences?

2. Look at the granite sample with the magnifying glass. Granites often have cavities called geodes, which are lined with good-sized crystals of the minerals that make up the granite. In particular, look for white quartz crystals and white or pink feldspar. You might also see thin, black flakes of mica.

3. Like many igneous rocks, granite is very hard. Because of this it is very useful for making roads and building. Granite is also used for headstones in graveyards. Try to spot examples of granite near where you live.

METAMORPHIC ROCK

When masses of magma rise upward through the Earth's crust, the rocks that they pass through are heated and subjected to intense pressure as they are squeezed aside. The rocks closest to the rising magma will be melted (making them igneous rocks).

Further away, the extreme heat and pressure alters the surrounding rocks

without actually melting them. This process is called thermal or contact metamorphism. Rocks altered in this way are called metamorphic, or 'changed-form' rocks. Marble, for example, is limestone that has been changed.

Metamorphic rocks may also be formed by the heat and pressure from the movement of plates. This happens particularly where mountain building is taking place. This form of metamorphosis is called regional metamorphism. Shale, a common sedimentary rock, is changed to slate by this process.

Did you know?

Some of the most valuable gemstones are produced by metamorphosis. Rubies and sapphires are formed by the action of molten magma on limestone, and garnets are often found in metamorphic rocks.

MARBLE AND SLATE

Find a sample of marble and a sample of slate, and have a look at their properties. Why do you think marble is so often used for decorating buildings? What do the layers in the slate tell you about the way it was formed? In what way do these layers make slate a useful rock?

Marble

Slate

MATERIALS
- a magnifying glass
- a piece of marble
- a piece of slate

METAMORPHIC BAKING

The ingredients you use for these chocolate chip cookies are like the minerals making up a rock. When you put the mixture in the oven the heat changes it, just as a rock is changed by contact metamorphosis. Nothing is removed from the mixture by the cooking process (except a little moisture) and nothing is added. In the same way, a rock is not altered chemically by metamorphosis, but the minerals in it are altered.

1. Ask an adult to turn the oven on to 190°C (375°F or Gas 5).

2. Cream the butter and sugar together until the mixture is light and fluffy.

3. Beat in the egg and vanilla essence.

4. Mix in the flour.

5. Stir in the chocolate chips.

6. Use the dessert spoon to drop spoonfuls of your mixture onto the greased baking sheet. Leave space between the mounds because they will spread when they cook.

7. Ask an adult to put the cookies in the oven. Bake for 10-15 minutes, or until they are golden brown. When the cookies are ready, ask an adult to take them out of the oven and lift them on to a wire rack to cool and harden.

SEDIMENTARY ROCK

Over long periods, rocks are broken up into small particles through the action of wind, water, ice and living things such as plants. These particles, called sediment, are carried away by the wind or by running water. Sand, clay and mud are all types of of sediment.

Sediment gathers at the mouths of rivers or at the bottom of shallow seas, anywhere in fact that the water current slows enough to let it settle. As layer upon layer of sediment is added over time, the weight of the upper layers begins to press down with immense force on the layers beneath. The massive weight squeezes out any water between the particles of rock.

Minerals that were dissolved in the water are left behind and these can act like a cement, holding the particles together. Eventually, the particles are compacted to form a solid mass of rock. Rocks formed in this way are called sedimentary rocks, because they are formed from sediments.

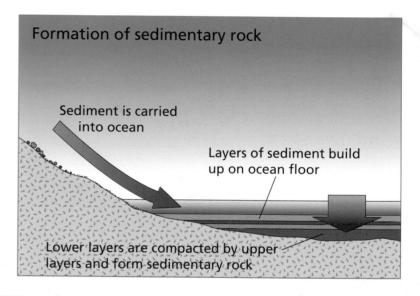

Formation of sedimentary rock

Sediment is carried into ocean

Layers of sediment build up on ocean floor

Lower layers are compacted by upper layers and form sedimentary rock

THE ACID TEST

Chalk is a type of limestone. It is made of calcite, one of an important group of minerals called carbonates. Carbonates all contain the elements carbon and oxygen. You can identify carbonates by carrying out an acid test.

MATERIALS
- a piece of chalk
- another small piece of rock
- vinegar

1. Drop a little vinegar on to any rock sample. If the surface of the rock fizzes it contains carbonate. You may have to look closely, as vinegar is a very weak acid.

2. Now try the test on some chalk. What happens? Why do you think this happens?

Chalk

Some sedimentary rocks are formed from the remains of once living creatures. Corals, tiny plants called diatoms and many shellfish extract calcium carbonate from seawater and use this to make their shells. After they die, they sink down to the bottom of the sea. Layer upon layer of the shelly remains pile up over millions of years, forming a deposit hundreds of metres deep. Once again pressure transforms the lower layers, compacting them into the rock known as limestone. Limestone is a very common sedimentary rock, found over large areas of the Earth.

MAKE YOUR OWN SANDSTONE

1. Ask an adult to cut the top half off the bottle.

2. Fill the measuring jug with sand up to the 400 ml mark, and pour the sand into the bottle.

MATERIALS

- a measuring jug
- plaster of Paris
- fine-grained sand
- 300 ml water
- a large, clear plastic bottle
- scissors
- a spoon or a stick

WARNING!

- Plaster of Paris becomes rock hard when it is set, so make sure you clear up any mess before this happens!

3. Measure the plaster of Paris in the same way, to the 300 ml mark, and mix in well with sand.

4. Add the water to the mixture and stir. The mixture should be fluid enough to stir but not too runny. Leave the mixture to harden overnight.

5. Ask an adult to cut away the bottle and remove your sandstone.

FOSSILS

Fossils are the remains of plants and animals that lived millions of years ago. Over time, the remains have been transformed to leave a record in the rocks of life in the distant past.

For a fossil to form, the animal or plant remains must be buried. An animal might drown in a river and be covered by silt. The soft parts of its body decay or are eaten before it is completely buried, but the hard parts, bones and teeth are left behind.

Fossils are often found in layers of sedimentary rock, where the remains

FOSSIL HUNTING

Fossils are most frequently found in sedimentary rocks, especially limestones and shales. Fossils of animals that lived in the ocean millions of years ago can sometimes be found in rocks on top of hills! A good place to look for fossils is on a pebbly beach. A guide to fossils will tell you where to look in your own area. If you live in a large town or city, you will find fossil collections in your local museum.

MAKE A FOSSIL

1. Mix ten parts of plaster of Paris with seven parts of water in one plastic pot. Stir to form a thick cream. Leave it to stand for a minute or two, but don't let it set completely!

2. Smear the object you are going to 'fossilize' with petroleum jelly, and press it gently into the surface of the plaster of Paris. Leave it until the plaster of Paris is completely set. This will take a day or so.

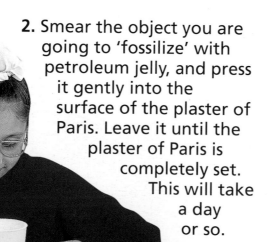

MATERIALS

- a shell, a leaf or a bone
- two cartons or pots
- plaster of Paris
- petroleum jelly
- water
- a spoon or a stick

WARNING!

- Plaster of Paris becomes rock hard when it is set, so make sure you clear up any mess before this happens!

The remains of this fossilized fish have been preserved in rock for millions of years. If you look at its mouth, you can see that the fish must have died while trying to swallow another, smaller fish!

bone or plant material as it decays. Eventually, the organic remains are entirely replaced by rock.

Sometimes the organic remains decay without being replaced by minerals, leaving a bone-shaped space like a mould. Minerals may eventually fill up the spaces where the bones once were, forming a cast. Millions of years later, erosion may expose the fossil on the surface.

got trapped in a layer of sediment. More layers piled on top of the bones, and sedimentary rock built up.

Over the course of thousands of years, the bones slowly dissolve away. Minerals dissolved in water replace the

3. Remove the object. The petroleum jelly will help it to come away easily. You will see an imprint of the object in the plaster of Paris.

4. The next step is to make a cast fossil. Smear some more petroleum jelly inside the mould.

5. Mix up a small amount of plaster of Paris in the other pot and pour it into the mould. Leave it to set.

6. Remove your plaster fossil from its mould.

Did you know?

Fossil forming is very rare. Probably only one in 20,000 of all the plant and animal species that have lived on the Earth have left a fossil record.

ROCK RESOURCES

Since the earliest times, human civilizations have made use of the wealth to be found in the rocks of the Earth. Valuable and useful metals, such as gold and silver, copper and iron; gemstones, such as diamonds and sapphires; and fossil fuels – coal, oil, and gas – have all shaped the development of our societies.

Coal, peat, oil and natural gas are together known as fossil fuels. Coal and peat were formed when plants decayed and became covered by sand and mud. The compressed material first became peat, and then turned to coal as it was pressed deeper into the Earth by layers of sediment. Oil and natural gas were also formed under layers of rock, sand and mud below the ocean. Heat and pressure turned decayed plants and animals into oil and gas.

Rocks that contain useful materials are called ores, and a mass of ore in one place is known as a deposit. Gold and silver are often found in veins, long branching deposits surrounded by rocks. When a large deposit of a useful material is found, a mine will be dug to get it out.

In the last hundred years we have mined more ore than in all of the rest of history. Coal, metals and all the Earth's other mineral resources cannot be replaced once they have been used up. It is vital that we learn to recycle as much as possible and find ways of conserving our fossil fuel stocks.

The seams of coal in this rock have become exposed over time, but they were formed underground from the remains of plants that lived between 250 and 350 million years ago.

THE RESOURCEFUL DETECTIVE

Rocks and the resources they hold are used all the time in your everyday life. Sources of power, such as oil and natural gas, are found in rocks. Oil is used to make plastics, too. Pottery, china, bricks and cement are all ceramics, made by heating clay and other raw materials. Glass is a ceramic, made from limestone and sand. Metals are used for everything from telephone cable and pipes to cutlery and door handles.

1. Look around your home and try to spot all the different uses of rocks and minerals.

2. Make a list of five of these items in your bedroom, five in the kitchen, and five used for building your home.

3. Make a chart with three columns. In the left hand column write the items you have chosen, such as teacup, or roof tiles.

4. In the second column, write what you think each item is made of, such as clay, brass, marble or slate.

5. In the third column, write the main rock resource the material comes from. A key would be metal ore. A plastic beaker would be oil.

Item	Material	Rock resource
storage box	plastic	oil
bottles	glass	limestone and sand

METEORITES

The oldest rocks found on the Earth did not originate on this planet. Meteorites are 'rocks from the sky', left over from the formation of the Solar System 4.5 billion years ago.

Before a meteorite enters the Earth's atmosphere it is called a meteoroid. Meteoroids can enter the atmosphere at speeds of up to 30 km/sec. Up to 90 per cent of the meteorite may be lost as it passes through the atmosphere.

The largest meteorite fragment known is the Hoba iron meteorite in Namibia. It is estimated to weigh 60 tonnes.

Almost all meteorites that reach the Earth's surface are stony meteorites, made up of minerals found in ordinary rocks, such as olivine and feldspar. Some stony meteorites are similar in their composition and appearance to volcanic rocks. However, these stony meteorites are likely to wear away with weathering. Because of this, we more often find meteorites composed of iron and nickel, even though only about six per cent of the meteorites that fall are of this type. A small number of meteorites are stony-irons, with roughly equal amounts of stony material and nickel-iron alloy.

METEOR WATCHING

Most meteors burn up completely in the atmosphere and never reach the ground. However, you might be able to see a meteor as it travels its fiery path through the Earth's atmosphere.

1. Consult a constellation chart which will tell you the best times of the year to see meteor showers in different parts of the sky, or constellations.

MATERIALS
- a starchart
- a pair of binoculars (optional)
- a garden chair
- warm clothes
- a notepad and pencil

LOOKING AT METEORITES

Many museums have one or more meteorites on display. If you want to see what one looks like, your nearest natural history, local history or geological museum would be good place to start.

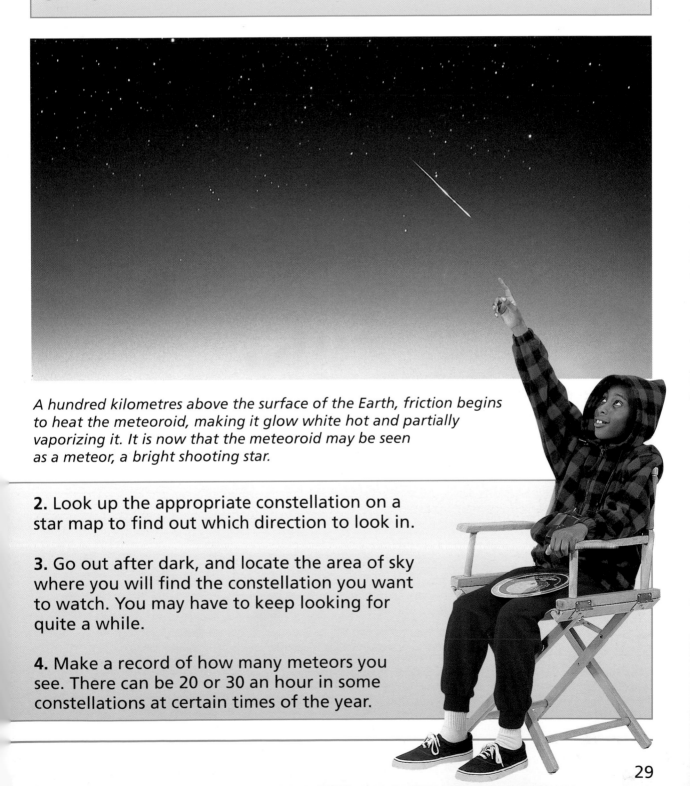

A hundred kilometres above the surface of the Earth, friction begins to heat the meteoroid, making it glow white hot and partially vaporizing it. It is now that the meteoroid may be seen as a meteor, a bright shooting star.

2. Look up the appropriate constellation on a star map to find out which direction to look in.

3. Go out after dark, and locate the area of sky where you will find the constellation you want to watch. You may have to keep looking for quite a while.

4. Make a record of how many meteors you see. There can be 20 or 30 an hour in some constellations at certain times of the year.

WEATHERING

Over time, even seemingly solid rocks can be broken down and dispersed by the forces of weathering and erosion. Weathering breaks the rock down into smaller fragments, and erosion, which we shall look at next, moves the fragments of rock from one place to another. The combined effect of weathering and erosion is known as denudation.

There are two types of weathering: physical (or mechanical) weathering, and chemical weathering. Both may be happening at the same time. Physical

These spires of sandstone in Utah in the USA were formed by centuries of weathering.

weathering includes the action of ice, known as frost shattering. As water freezes, it expands, opening up cracks in the rock surface. Extremes of temperature, such as those found in deserts, can cause rocks to expand and contract. This results in flaking at the surface. Rocks loosened by physical weathering of all kinds may roll down a slope to form a pile of shattered fragments called a scree.

Chemical weathering changes the minerals that make up the rock. The most common agent of chemical weathering is rainwater. Carbon dioxide gas in the atmosphere dissolves in the rain forming a weak acid called carbonic acid that slowly dissolves some of the minerals in the rock.

Acid rain, caused by various pollutants in the atmosphere, contains acids that are stronger than the usual carbonic acid. Many statues and buildings show the damaging effects of acid rain. Minerals in granite are dissolved by the acids and limestone, one of the carbonate rocks, is particularly vulnerable.

ICEBREAKER

Rocks that are exposed to freezing and thawing are broken up as the water in their cracks expands when it turns to ice.

1. Wet the clay and roll it into a ball.

2. Place the ball in a plastic bag and put it in the freezer. Leave the clay in the freezer overnight.

3. Take the ball out of the freezer. Its surface should be slightly cracked and broken.

4. Wet it again, taking care not to close up the cracks that have formed, and put it back in the freezer for another night. When you take it out, what has happened to the cracks?

MATERIALS

- clay
- a plastic bag
- water
- a freezer

EROSION

The rock fragments formed by weathering may not stay in the same place for very long. More likely they will be carried away by the wind, by running water or even by moving ice. The movement of rock fragments from one place to another is called erosion.

Wind erosion is most obvious in dry, desert areas. In regions where there is no sheltering vegetation, the wind can strip off dry soils. Only small particles are carried by the wind, but the force of flowing water, or hydraulic action, can move much larger fragments. The faster the water flows, the larger the fragments it can shift. Water from rainfall or melting snow runs downhill, taking particles of rock and soil with it. Rocks carried along in the water are gradually reduced in size, and become smooth and rounded as they bounce along the river bed and against each other. This process is called attrition, and it happens also to smaller, windblown particles.

Most of the power of wind, water and ice to strip away rocks comes from the abrasive effect of the rock fragments they carry. This is called corrasion. In deserts, windblown sand scours rock surfaces into fantastic, honeycomb shapes. Rocks carried by a river current widen the actual river bed by knocking out more material along the way. Along shorelines, the tides grind sand and pebbles against rock surfaces.

Ice is the most powerful of the erosive forces. All over the world, the effects of ice can be seen in great valleys carved out by moving glaciers during the ice ages. Huge boulders can be carried hundreds of kilometres by glaciers. This glacier is in Alaska, USA.

Did you know?
The wind can carry dust across the Atlantic Ocean from Europe and Africa to the islands of the Caribbean.

A LITTLE LANDSCAPE

1. Fill the seed tray with the soil and scatter the stones over the surface.

2. Take your seed tray outside and leave it in a windy place.

3. Take a look at the seed tray after a day or so. Is all the soil still there? What has happened to the soil around the rocks?

4. Now raise the seed tray at one end by resting it on the block. Don't raise it so much that all the rocks roll off! Rest the bottom of the seed tray in the other tray. Top up with more soil if need be.

5. Trickle water on to the raised end of the tray using the watering can. What happens to the soil as the water runs through it?

6. Refill your tray with soil, and replace any stones if necessary. Add some grass seed, and water well.

7. Leave your grass until it has grown for a few weeks, but keep it watered. Then repeat steps **4** and **5**. What happens?

FROM ROCK TO SOIL

Dig deep enough beneath any soil and you will reach rock. As we have just seen, rocks are continually being pounded, broken and dispersed by the forces of weathering and erosion. This weathering of rocks produces a mixture of minerals. Over time a seemingly solid rock, such as granite, is turned into clay and sand. The destruction of the rock is the first stage in the creation of soil.

When plants and other living things make a home in the fragmented rocks, they begin to produce soil. In fact, although you may need to dig down one hundred metres or more to hit bedrock, only the topmost layer containing living organisms is called soil. The depth of this topmost layer varies from place to place, from five metres in warm, moist areas to less than one centimetre in very dry, cold places.

Soil particles are grouped in three main sizes: sand, silt and clay. Light soils may contain up to 50 per cent sand, the largest of the soil particles. Sandy soils drain well because water can pass easily between the large particles. Soil that is too sandy will not hold water well and tends to dry out.

On the other hand, clay soils, which have the smallest particles, can almost stop water draining through them altogether when they are wet and the ground becomes waterlogged. If you have ever handled a lump of wet clay you will know how heavy and sticky it can be.

SOIL GRADING

What is the composition of the soil in your area? You can tell a lot just by handling it. If there is a lot of sand in the soil it will feel gritty. Silty soils will roll smoothly between your fingers. Clay soils will be sticky when wet, but smooth when dry.

MATERIALS
• a spade
• soil
• a large-holed sieve
• a fine mesh sieve
• a large piece of paper or cloth

1. Dig up a sample of soil.

2. Spread it out on a large piece of paper or cloth, and break up the larger lumps.

3. Put your sample into the large-holed sieve and shake it so that the small and medium-sized particles fall through. Larger rocks and coarse soil particles will be left behind.

Plants draw nourishment and grow in the soil, and we depend on this for much of our food. Soils with fairly equal mixtures of sand, clay and humus (decaying plant and animal material) are best for growing crops.

4. Take the soil that has fallen through the sieve and shake it through the fine mesh. Medium-grade soil will be left in the sieve and fine-grade soil will fall through.

5. Compare the amounts of each type of soil. How much of your soil is coarse, how much medium, and how much fine?

THE LIVING EARTH

Living things play a part in soil creation from the beginning. Lichens and mosses can colonize bare rock surfaces. They produce acids that eat into the rock surface, releasing the minerals that plants need to grow. The mosses and lichens also help to trap tiny wind-blown particles in cracks and depressions in the rock surface. Over long periods of time, soil begins to form.

After hundreds, perhaps thousands, of years enough soil builds up on the rock surface to allow larger plants, such as grasses, to take root. Plants need nutrients to grow, and they grow roots to do this. Plant roots can exert a tremendous force and are capable of breaking rocks into smaller pieces. Eventually, where once there were bare rocks, a forest may grow, complete with the range of plants and animals it supports.

Spiders and other small hunters are often the first animals to colonize a rock surface. They hide in the cracks and crevices, catching insects that are blown on to the rocks. Bacteria, fungi,

Soil is an active, constantly changing material that may teem with life. Animal remains add to the growing collection of organic matter that forms a vital part of the soil.

and other decomposers break down the wastes and remains of other organisms and return their matter to the soil. The result is that vital soil ingredient humus. Humus makes up less than five per cent of the volume of an average soil, but this natural fertilizer provides growing plants with an essential source of nutrients.

A SOIL ORGANISM SURVEY

1. Put the soil and leaf litter in the sieve, enough to fill it half way up.

2. Line the tray with paper, and rest the sieve on supports over the tray.

3. Place the desk lamp so the light shines onto the sieve. Many soil creatures try to avoid the light. They will move deeper into the soil sample and many will fall through the sieve on to the paper in the tray below.

4. Check the tray a few times over the next hour or so. The magnifying glass will be handy for examining the smaller specimens.

5. Try the survey with samples from other areas and at different times of the year. Is there a difference in the number of creatures you see?

SOIL PROFILES

Most soils can be divided into distinct layers, or horizons. The topmost layer, made up of fallen leaves and other decomposing material, is sometimes called the O horizon. The next layer, called the A horizon, is where most of the organic material is found. Many different organisms will be found living in this layer. Rainwater dissolves minerals from this layer and carries them to the next layer down, a process called leaching.

The next layer, the B horizon, contains a great deal of decomposed organic material combined with minerals. A great many organisms make their home in this layer as well. Plant roots penetrate down to the B horizon in search of the minerals leached from the A horizon.

The C horizon is made up of rock fragments and soil. At the base of the soil layers is the bedrock, the R horizon. Under most conditions, plants and soil organisms are absent from the lowest layers. The total vertical pattern, including all the horizons, is called the soil profile.

This diagram shows the layers of a typical soil profile. The horizons of different soils may vary in the amounts of organic matter, thickness, colour, clay content, or other features. The actual depth of these layers and the exact mixture of minerals and organic material in each depends on the climate and on the rocks from which the soil was formed.

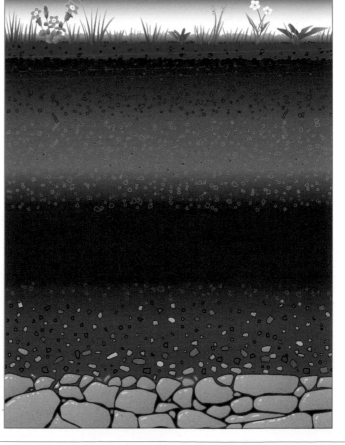

O horizon

A horizon

B horizon

C horizon

R horizon

Autumn leaves, part of the O horizon, will soon disappear into the A horizon as they decompose.

PROFILE IN A BOTTLE

MATERIALS

- small stones or gravel
- sand
- soil
- leaves
- a large plastic bottle or jar

1. If you are using a plastic bottle, ask an adult to cut the top third off and discard.

2. Put a layer of gravel in the bottom of the bottle or jar, followed by a layer of sand. These are your C and B horizons.

3. Now add a layer of sand mixed with soil, and then another layer of soil. This will be your A horizon.

4. Scatter a few leaves on top to act as your O horizon.

39

SOIL GROUPS

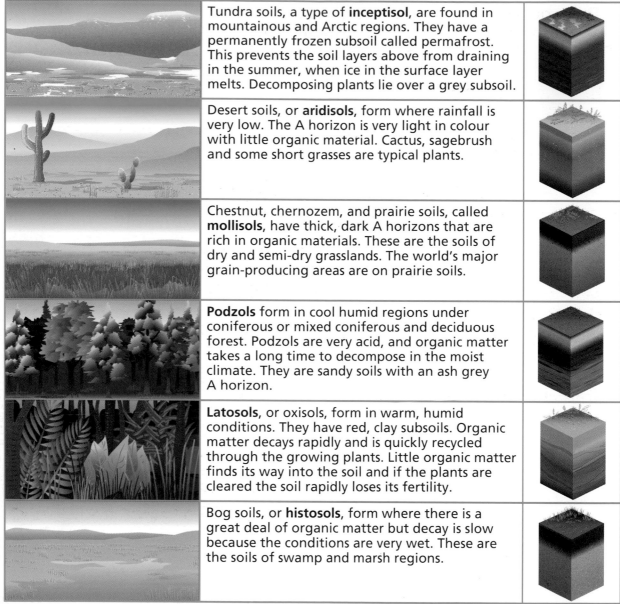

Tundra soils, a type of **inceptisol**, are found in mountainous and Arctic regions. They have a permanently frozen subsoil called permafrost. This prevents the soil layers above from draining in the summer, when ice in the surface layer melts. Decomposing plants lie over a grey subsoil.

Desert soils, or **aridisols**, form where rainfall is very low. The A horizon is very light in colour with little organic material. Cactus, sagebrush and some short grasses are typical plants.

Chestnut, chernozem, and prairie soils, called **mollisols**, have thick, dark A horizons that are rich in organic materials. These are the soils of dry and semi-dry grasslands. The world's major grain-producing areas are on prairie soils.

Podzols form in cool humid regions under coniferous or mixed coniferous and deciduous forest. Podzols are very acid, and organic matter takes a long time to decompose in the moist climate. They are sandy soils with an ash grey A horizon.

Latosols, or oxisols, form in warm, humid conditions. They have red, clay subsoils. Organic matter decays rapidly and is quickly recycled through the growing plants. Little organic matter finds its way into the soil and if the plants are cleared the soil rapidly loses its fertility.

Bog soils, or **histosols**, form where there is a great deal of organic matter but decay is slow because the conditions are very wet. These are the soils of swamp and marsh regions.

The world's soils are divided into different groups according to the different climates and conditions in which they form.

Red and yellow soils, or ultisols, are similar to the grey-brown soils but have redder colours. Mixed deciduous and coniferous forests grow on these soils.

Alluvial soils are deposited along the banks of rivers and streams. They do not have separate horizons. They are among the world's most fertile soils as new material is constantly being deposited by the river.

INVESTIGATING SOIL TYPES

This would make a good project to do with a group of friends. You could investigate whether or not the soil was different in various parts of your community by having people bring in samples from their gardens.

MATERIALS

- large glass or plastic jars
- soil samples
- water
- a ruler

1. Put a different sample into each jar. Fill the jars with soil so that they are about half full.

2. Fill the rest of the jar to about three-quarters full with water and give it a good shake. Leave the jars to settle overnight.

3. Next day have a look at your samples. At the bottom will be a layer of the heaviest sand and stones. Next will come the lighter grains of sand. In the middle will be a fine layer of silt. Above this might be cloudy layer of water with fine clay particles suspended in it. Floating on the top will be the humus and any organic materials.

4. Measure the depth of each layer and compare your different soil types. How does the amount of organic material vary from one type to another?

5. Try to collect soil samples when you or someone you know goes to another part of the country, and compare them to your own.

NATURAL GARDENERS

About half the volume of a good soil is made up of air spaces. These spaces allow water to be stored in the soil. Nutrients from the humus are dissolved in the water, making them available to plants.

The tunnelling activities of moles, although a nuisance, are very good for soil. The tunnels make air spaces, allowing water to penetrate the soil and reduce erosion. Moles are well adapted to life underground, with earholes covered against dirt, strong front feet for digging, and a sensitive snout for finding food in the soil.

MAKE A WORMERY

You can make a wormery to watch earthworms doing their job of mixing and aerating the soil.

1. Fill the jar about 3/4 full with layers of sand, peat and soil. Water it well, but don't make it too wet or your earthworms might drown.

2. Put the earthworms on top of the soil and cover them with leaves.

3. Cover the wormery with the cloth. Earthworms don't like the light. Inspect your wormery every day or so to see how the worms are doing. Keep the soil moist.

MATERIALS
- a large glass or plastic jar
- sand
- peat
- garden soil
- leaves
- a dark cloth
- ten large earthworms

Soil-burrowing animals, such as ants and earthworms, make tunnels through the soil along which air and water can travel. At the same time they mix the humus from the top layer of the soil with the sand, silt, and clay in the lower layers.

Most of the creatures that live in the soil are decomposers – nature's recycling squad, breaking down the remains of dead plants, animals and animal wastes for re-use by a new generation of plants. Tiny animals, such as protonurans, springtails, and bristletails feed on fallen leaves and other material, slowly nibbling it away. Woodlice, slugs and snails are also at home in the leaf litter. Mini-hunters, such as spiders, beetles and centipedes, will also be found in the soil as they come to prey on decomposers.

4. After a few days you should see how the worms begin to mix the soil as they tunnel through it. This is what they do naturally, breaking down and redistributing old plant material for re-use as a natural fertilizer, and helping air get into the soil.

5. When you've finished with your wormery, remember to put these valuable natural gardeners back where you found them!

THE HUMAN FACTOR

Overgrazing has caused desertification in this area of East Africa. The Sahara Desert in Africa is spreading south at an alarming rate as the topsoil in the surrounding regions is lost, due to lack of plant cover.

One of the most dramatic ways the Earth's rocks and soils are being altered is through the activities of humans. Natural erosion, which has produced the landforms we see today, carries on very slowly. Humans speed up the process of erosion by changing the environment in different ways, for instance by cutting down forests and leaving the soil exposed.

Overgrazing by animal herds and unsound farming methods also accelerate the process of erosion. Plant cover is vital in holding back the effects of erosion by wind and water.

Farmland with vast areas of a single crop stretching into the distance are not natural. These artificial landscapes,

> ### Did you know?
> Each year the world s desert regions increase in size by over 50,000 square kilometres. Between 1950 and 1990, 20 per cent of the world s topsoil

maintained by pesticides and fertilizers, are deserts for wild plants and animals.

There are many ways to combat accelerated erosion. For example, belts of trees can act as windbreaks, helping to prevent loss of the topsoil in vulnerable areas. Trees on slopes prevent loss by water erosion as well. It may take several thousand years for just a metre of soil to form. For this reason, and because we depend so much on healthy soils for our food, it is vital that we look after our soils.

THE GOOD EARTH

How healthy are the soils in your area?

1. Ask permission to take a small sample of soil from a field of wheat or other crop, or from a vegetable patch. If permission is given, be careful not to disturb the growing plants. Get samples from wasteland, from a garden and from a forest if you can.

2. Put each sample in a separate tray. Remove any plants already growing in the sample.

3. Sow a few wild flower seeds in each tray and water them gently.

4. Take care of the growing seeds. Measure the amount of water you give them so that each sample is treated in the same way.

5. Record how the plants grow. Which soil sample produces the best results? Why do you think this is?

MATERIALS

- soil samples
- shallow trays
- a packet of wild flower seeds
- a trowel and fork
- a measuring jug
- a watering can

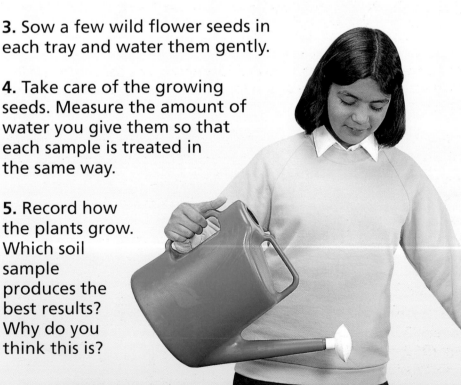

GLOSSARY

Asthenosphere The soft, partially melted upper layer of the mantle, 70 to 260 km beneath the Earth's surface, upon which the plates move.

Basalt A fine-grained igneous rock. Basalts make up 90 per cent of volcanic rocks. Cooling basalt forms characteristic hexagonal columns.

Bedrock The solid and unweathered rock beneath a layer of soil and weathered rock.

Continental crust The part of the Earth's crust that constitutes the continents. It is composed largely of granite rocks and is on average 33 km thick, although it may reach up to 70 km under mountains. It is less dense than, and therefore floats on, the oceanic crust.

Core The central part of the Earth that begins about 2,900 km beneath the surface. It is divided into a liquid outer core consisting of a mixture of iron, nickel and sulphur, and a solid inner core composed of a dense alloy of nickel and iron.

Crust The outer layer of the Earth, between 6 and 70 km thick. It is divided into continental crust and oceanic crust.

Erosion The wearing away of the land surface by the action of debris carried by agents such as glaciers, rivers, winds and ocean currents.

Fault A fracture in the crust along which the rocks have moved. Most faults occur in groups called fault zones.

Fold A buckling of rocks in the crust owing to their being compressed by earth movements, such as a collision of continents.

Fossil fuels Fuels, such as coal, oil and natural gas, that have been created from the remains of living organisms by the effects of heat and pressure within the Earth.

Granite A coarse-grained, igneous rock that is the basic constituent of the continental crust.

Limestone A sedimentary rock formed by the accumulation on the seabed of the skeletons and shells of marine organisms.

Lithosphere The rigid upper layer of the Earth, about 75 km thick, consisting of the crust and the solid, upper mantle. It 'floats' on the asthenosphere.

Magma Molten rock found more than 16 km below the Earth's surface. Magma that reaches the surface through volcanoes or fissures in the ground is called lava.

Mantle The part of the Earth's interior lying between the crust and the core, roughly between 30 and 2,900 km beneath the surface.

Meteor A streak of light seen in a clear night sky, when a small interplanetary rock fragment burns up in the Earth's upper atmosphere as a result of friction. The fragments themselves are known as meteoroids. Meteoroids that survive the journey through the atmosphere to land on the Earth are known as meteorites.

Mineral A naturally-occurring chemical element or compound with a definite chemical composition. Rocks are composed of mixtures of minerals.

Oceanic crust The part of the Earth's crust, between 6 and 16 kilometres thick, that lies beneath the ocean floor. It is composed largely of basalt.

Ore A naturally-occurring mineral from which metal or other useful materials can be extracted.

Weathering The breakdown of rock on or near the Earth's surface. This can be done by chemical processes, such as the dissolving of rock by water. It can also be done by mechanical processes. such as the splitting of rocks by temperature changes.

FURTHER INFORMATION

BOOKS

The Changing Landscape, Dougal Dixon (Wayland, 1990)

Focus on Rocks and Fossils, Ray Oliver (Hamlyn, 1993)

How the Earth Works, John Farndon (Dorling Kindersley, 1993)

Planet Earth, Fiona Watt (Usborne, 1991)

The Story of the Earth, F. W. Dunning (Natural History Museum, 1991)

Super Science Book of Rocks and Soils, Robert Snedden (Wayland, 1994)

ANSWERS TO QUESTIONS

Answers to questions posed in the projects.

Page 9 As the ice melts and runs off the block of wood, the weight on the block is lessened and it rises higher in the water again.

Page 19 A piece of granite is much heavier than a similarly-sized one of pumice. No bubbles of gas were trapped in granite when it formed. Granite cooled slowly inside the Earth, forming large crystals, which can be clearly seen.

Pumice cooled rapidly in the air, and no crystals are visible to the eye. The pumice has a smooth texture, compared to the coarse texture of the granite.

Page 20 Marble is an attractive, hard-wearing rock that can be polished to a shiny, attractive appearance. Pure limestones produce brilliant white marble. Muddier limestones give marbles with coloured streaks and patches.

Slate is formed from shale, a sedimentary rock that was laid down in layers. Slate is a tough, waterproof rock that splits readily into thin sheets that can be used for roofing.

Page 22 Chalk is a limestone rock, and so you should see some fizzing as bubbles of carbon dioxide are given off.

Page 31 The cracks in the clay should have opened wider. More water will get into the cracks and open them up further as it freezes and expands.

Page 33 Some of the soil may have blown away, but the rocks should have acted like a windbreak and protected the soil downwind from wind erosion. Many of the finer soil particles will be washed down the slope by the water, just like a stream or river eroding a landscape. Plants play an important role in erosion control. Their roots bind the soil particles, helping prevent it from being washed or blown away. Once the grass has grown, less soil should wash away as you pour water down the slope.

Page 37 You should find more organisms in the soil and leaf litter from a woodland floor than from a well-trodden path where the soil has become compacted, making it difficult for animals to burrow through it. In winter you will find fewer organisms. Many overwinter in the form of eggs to escape the harsher conditions.

Page 45 The soil you take from the field may produce the best results if fertilizers have been used on the crop. The soil from the wasteland will proably be poor in nutrients and therefore give poor results.

INDEX